Synching
Mind,
Heart
& Life

where
are my
emotions
now

Thirtysix.org

Where Are My Emotions Now?

Synching Mind, Heart & Life

ISBN 9781091221864

Published by:
Thirtysix.org
22 Yitzchak Road
Telzstone, Kiryat Yearim
Israel   90838

Dedicated to
all the people
who suffer
relentlessly
and in need
of a way back
to life.

WHERE ARE MY emotions NOW? This is not a question that most people ask themselves during the course of a day. It's not even a question that most people think about during their entire life. It's just assumed that they are where they always are and belong, here and now.

For depressed people, the opposite is true. Their emotions are anywhere BUT in the here and now. They walk outside on a beautiful sunny day and experience only gray clouds. At a simcha, when they should be feeling light and joyous, they feel sad and burdened, and the happiness around them makes them feel even MORE sad and more burdened.

There's a lot of FEAR too. It's scary not to be in control, and it's scariest of ALL when we're not in control of OURSELF. If you can't control yourself, then what CAN you control? And if you can't control yourself, how can you possibly be happy when you want to be, or sad when you have to be?

Life is full of suffering, whether we are rich or poor, healthy or sick, popular or lonely. Everyone involuntarily suffers in some way and at some point. It's a characteristic of being human, and a necessity of being Jewish.[1] It's just the HOW of suffering that varies from person to person.

The rabbis phrased it like this:

According to the suffering is the reward. (Pirkei Avos 5:23)

Many prefer to rephrase the statement as "According to the EFFORT is the reward," because it sounds more palatable. Although not untrue, it is less accurate because the original Aramaic word is "tzara," which means "pain."

Ironically, the English equivalent is more accurate: No pain, no gain. It acknowledges that pain is not only part of life, but important for ac-

---

[1] Brochos 5a.

complishment in it. The goal is not the pain, but we need to recognize that many goals are accomplished only THROUGH pain.

That's okay, as long as the end result can justify it. For example, business people will put up with a lot of suffering—extra schooling, long hours of work, reduced family time—because they believe it will eventually lead to success. Athletes week in and week out put themselves through terrible pain, including grueling training and stressful competition, because it can lead to victory and rich endorsements.

The problem is not suffering. It is rather the UNPLANNED suffering, the UNCONTROLLABLE suffering, the WASTEFUL suffering, or at least what appears to us at the time to be suffering that just doesn't make sense. That kind of suffering gets in the way of our life, until we find out otherwise, later on:

> A man died and found himself standing before the Heavenly Tribunal. As he waited to see what would become of him, he noticed that the place looked somewhat like a train station, and it appeared as if a train were slowly approaching down the tracks.

"What's THAT?" he asked the angel next to him, as a sparkling white train pulled into the station.

"Those are all the mitzvos you performed in your lifetime."

"Really?" The train stopped and all kinds of white angels hopped off and climbed onto what seemed to be one side of a large scale, weighing it down. For the moment, the man felt assured of a place in heaven.

But before he could comment, he saw another train coming from the distance. Confused, he asked the angel, "And what's THAT?"

"THAT," the angel said ominously, "are all your sins!"

The man gulped, as a long black train pulled into the station and stopped. He became quite concerned when he saw how long the train was, and how many black angels ran off it and onto the scale, weighing it down more and more until the sins outweighed the mitzvos. The man now anticipated a long and painful stay in Gehinnom.[2]

---

[2] Purgatory.

Just when he thought all was lost, he saw a THIRD train make its way towards the Tribunal, and he became even more confused.

"A THIRD train?" he asked the angel.

"Oh yes!" the angel replied excitedly. "That train carries all your suffering!"

"My suffering?" the man repeated to himself, as he watched in awe as a beautiful GOLD train pulled in and came to a stop. It wasn't long, but gold angels floated off the train and onto the scale to add weight to the side of the mitzvos. He waited nervously for the final verdict.

One gold angel, another gold angel...each one slowly pushed the scale farther down in his favor. When it became very close, he was unable to control himself any longer and almost involuntarily yelled out, "MORE SUFFERING! MORE SUFFERING!"

One of the things that allows average people to COPE with THEIR bouts of suffering is the times they DON'T suffer.[3] In between life's painful moments they usually have a number of happy

---

[3] This is true for those suffering from psychological depression. Clinical depression works differently and its management usually requires professional assistance.

moments, joyful moments, moments of satisfaction that come from important things, like personal accomplishment for example.

And although they may CONSCIOUSLY forget what those moments felt like when they hit emotional snags, all these moments are stored in the UNCONSCIOUS. They remain there for a very long time and contribute to an almost unconscious sense of a good quality of life.

It's impossible NOT to lose in life at one time or another. Even the greatest do so at certain points. But winning MORE than losing allows people to still feel like winners, even after they have lost. It's what encourages them to keep trying to win all over again.

But people who continue to lose may begin to view themselves as chronic losers. When they perceive that they have lost more than they have won, their past victories may seem imaginary, fleeting, and no longer relevant. They begin to EXPECT to lose, which ends up being a self-fulfilling prophecy, and then they will have no way to cope naturally with their suffering.

Something else that allows non-depressed people to bounce back from loss, in whatever form it takes, is that their emotions are in synch. Because they can feel happy when it is time to be happy, they can be sad when it is time to be sad.

The fact that their emotions are on the same page as their mind enables them to feel that they can afford to be hurt when it's necessary.

Depressed people can't feel joy even when they're having it because their emotions are somewhere else. They can SEE that they're experiencing what should be a joyous occasion, but the emotions necessary to FEEL and CONFIRM it just aren't there. They're somewhere else, busy, in another place, DISTRACTED, feeling other and inappropriate emotions, such as sadness or fear.

This lack of emotional synch only compounds their negative feelings. The lack of emotional control scares them even more, making them feel cheated out of pleasure that is rightfully theirs. How could they not feel hopeless and more depressed when that happens day in and day out?

Ironically, it is the same when they want to feel sad but can't. People WANT to mourn the loss of a close relative or friend. It is normal and healthy, but when they feel emotionally numb at such moments, they wonder, "What's WRONG with me?" They then become even more scared and down on themselves. After all, they can SEE what they're supposed to be feeling, so why can't they actually feel it?

Everyday prayer can also be an occasion for

AWOL[4] emotions, as one person describes:

> Praying to God, especially Shemoneh Esrei, is like entering the Kodesh Kodashim, the Holy of Holies. It's a time that you come face to face with God, so to speak, and therefore a time when you want to think only about what is relevant to such a holy moment. But that is exactly when I start to have bothersome and intrusive thoughts. If I have the same thoughts during other times of the day, I might not even pay attention to them. But during Shemoneh Esrei? It is especially disturbing to me because I can't stop them from coming, and it defiles my prayer. I get so upset sometimes that I even lose track of where I am in prayer. How can the whole experience not be disappointing, and depressing? I end up feeling robbed of such an important opportunity to connect to God!

How true, sort of. Yes, an important opportunity to connect to God has been squandered, but not because of the intrusive thoughts per se. They certainly played a significant role in the unfortunate chain of events, but not the MAIN one.

---

[4] Absent without leave.

THESE THOUGHTS were just a diversion, something like that person down the street, for example, who pretends to faint in order to distract the attention of passers-by so that someone else can rob the bank at the other end of the street.

The perfect prayer requires both intellect and emotions to be on the same page, literally. If the intellect is not there, the emotions certainly won't be either. But the person will not notice or care, because it will be as if he didn't pray at all. This is the case with many people who go "elsewhere" while they are in shul.[5]

If the intellect is there—meaning that person has come to pray and connect to God—but his or her emotions are not also there, then he or she will have a unfulfilling experience. The feeling will be one of having been cheated of a spiritual opportunity, and it will be disappointing, depressing, and frustrating.

This is why the rabbis of the Mishnaic[6] Era used to spend an hour preparing for prayer.[7] They used that time to align their emotions with their intellect, so that they would be 100 percent there

---

[5] Synagogue.
[6] They were the authors of the recorded Mishnah, the essence of Torah Sh'b'al Peh, the Oral Law of Torah. The Talmud expands on the teachings of the Mishnah.
[7] Brochos 32b.

when talking to God. You wouldn't take a personal phone call while talking to your CEO, so why take a personal thought while talking to THE CEO of Creation?

If you think about all your most memorable experiences, you might recall how your emotions were in synch with your intellect. They were there, in the moment, undistracted, allowing you to FEEL what you THOUGHT and experienced, and there is NOTHING more real than that.

Because at the end of the day, that is what counts most, REALITY. We want to FEEL that we exist, not just KNOW it. And for THAT, we need our emotions to work together with our intellect, whether to feel happy or sad, as reality requires. Life is a battle for sure, and you have a MUCH greater chance of winning it if you understand this idea, and how to use it to your advantage.

where are my emotions now

one

know thine enemy

THERE IS A Torah mitzvah to HATE Amalek,[1] which is interesting since Amalek went to war against us only once, and the Egyptian people enslaved us for 116 years! The only reason the Egyptians didn't wipe us out, as Amalek tried to do, was because they preferred to squeeze us for

---

[1] As enumerated by the Rambam, there are three mitzvos: (#598) Remember what Amalek did to the Jewish people (Devarim 27:17); (#599) wipe out the descendants of Amalek (Devarim 25:19); and (#600) do not forget Amalek's atrocities and ambush on our journey from Egypt in the desert (Devarim 25:19). The Sfas Emes said that the command was to fully hate Amalek, rather than perform any actual action (Shemos, Zachor 646).

every last drop of life in order to build monuments to themselves.

And yet, not only is there NOT a mitzvah to hate the Egyptians, there is even a mitzvah to be nice to them:

> Egypt is destined to bring a gift to Moshiach, and he will not want to accept it from them. But the Holy One, blessed is He, will tell him, "Accept it from them, because they gave hospitality to My children in Egypt." Immediately "nobles shall come out of Egypt [bringing gifts]" (Tehillim 68:32). (Pesachim 118b)

An Egyptian is allowed to eventually convert and join the Jewish people. An Amaleki cannot. There has never been a mitzvah to take revenge against the Egyptians for what they did to us, but even God has sworn to be at war against Amalek until his end.[2]

True, as Rashi explains, Amalek brought special attention to himself because he cooled the Jewish people down.[3] He was the first one to attack the Jewish people after they left Egypt, dampening what had been an otherwise tri-

---

[2] Shemos 17:16.
[3] Rashi, Devarim 25:18.

umphant exodus from Egypt. Thanks to Amalek, the Jewish people no longer believed themselves invincible.

True to his name, Amalek caused doubt. His name in gematria is equal to that of "suffek," the Hebrew word for "doubt."[4] That is what Amalek does best—mess with people's minds by using "hester panim" to make them question God's involvement in their life.

Hester panim, the hiding of God's face so to speak, is built into history. For the sake of free will, it is necessary, as the Torah warns:

> My fury will rage against them on that day, and I will abandon them and hide My face from them, and they will be consumed, and many evils and troubles will befall them, and they will say on that day, "Is it not because our God is no longer among us, that these evils have befallen us?" And I will hide My face on that day BECAUSE OF ALL THE EVIL THEY COMMITTED when they turned to other gods. (Devarim 31:17-18)

It doesn't mean that God actually goes away.

---

4 "Amalek," spelled Ayin-Mem-Lamed-Kuf = 70+40+30+100 = 240; "suffek," spelled Samech-Peh-Kuf = 60+80+100 = 240.

He can't. If He did, Creation would go with Him. It doesn't mean that He stops running history. It can't run any other way. It just means that God runs history in a way that gives people the impression that He has gone away, or at least backed off from being involved in the affairs of man.

Consequently history takes on the appearance of randomness. Good people SEEM to suffer, and bad people SEEM to act with impunity. Honest people SEEM to lose out while cheaters SEEM to prosper. How could a JUST God ever allow THAT to happen?

All this, however, is only the way it APPEARS. In truth God never ceases to be just, even when we lose the right to see His justice at work. He simply veils it, so that what happens can easily fool those who do not care to understand more deeply what is going on.

For Amalek, the situation could not be more ideal. The rules of engagement force God to work mysteriously, and this allows Amalek to make people think that God is not involved in their life. It makes God appear absent, or at least unreliable, causing people to mistakenly and dangerously turn their back on God, with the result that God actually turns His back on them.

Amalek has many weapons to use, depending on the kind of battle and whom he is fighting.

In the first battle at Refidim he used astrology.[5] In later wars he used more conventional military equipment and weapons of mass destruction. In the Holocaust he used gas chambers or worked us to death.

The means of destruction may vary from attack to attack, but the goal is ALWAYS the same: yaiush, abandonment. He wants people to give up, to give up on God, to give up on good, to give up on true meaning. It doesn't matter what form this abandonment takes, just as long as it happens.

So if a person is having a blast in life, but one that clearly indicates that he does not believe in God or Torah, that is a victory for Amalek. If he can make a person lose hope in life, he has won another battle. If he can aggravate people and cause them to focus away from their godly task, then Amalek has cause to celebrate. As long as someone is held back from being God's partner in the perfection of Creation, Amalek is ahead of the game.

And he's not stupid—far from it. He knows how to set events in motion so that by the time the final one affects a person and does its damage, his tracks have been covered. No one is the

---

[5] Midrash Tanchuma, Beshallach 28.

wiser, and he is the winner.

Just ask yourself one question: How DIS-TRACTED am I at important SPIRITUAL moments? How many times do I do something, or forget to do something, and it ends up distracting me at an important moment when I am trying to better connect to GOD?

Sometimes when it comes to PHYSICAL moments, Amalek not only doesn't distract us, but he does whatever he can to help us stay focused. Achieving material success works in his favor because, as the Talmud says, few are spiritually capable of eating from two "tables" at the same time.[6] It's usually one or the other.

Some simple examples of Amalek at work follow.

There is a special blessing to say after using the bathroom that thanks God for all the miracles necessary to allow our body to function. What person who values health and believes that God is responsible for it wouldn't want to take this blessing seriously?

Yet time and time again people find themselves at the end of the blessing, not quite sure how they got there. The whole blessing takes less than a minute to say WITH intention, yet some-

---

[6] Brochos 5b.

times it seems to pass in mere seconds, frustrating the person who had wanted to be sincere.

Due to the magnitude of the problem, laminated cards with this blessing have been printed. These cards can be posted on a wall to help people focus on the words as they say them. And yet even with this, too many find that their mind wanders unless they work really hard to keep it focused on the brochah.

Or someone is trying to focus on the blessings of the Shemoneh Esrai, and might be doing a decent job of it when a cell phone goes off, breaking the concentration. Even the slightest beep that tells a phone owner that a message or email has come in can throw others off their dovening.

And then, as the emotions of people who have been interrupted shift to frustration, or even anger towards the person who forgot to turn off his phone before entering shul, they lose track of where they left off. This can compound the frustration as they try to recall which blessing was the last one they said so they can continue from where they were.

Technology is wonderful and truly enhances the quality of life. The downside is that life has become INCREDIBLY distracting because of it, more than ever before, at least during peacetime. War is also extremely distracting, but the distraction is more obvious and therefore less spiritually dangerous, as well as more excusable.

But for the time being the world is at peace, and there is nary a day that some new technology doesn't come onto the market and people rush to buy it. Bells and whistles? There are so many today that unless you cut yourself off from all of it, or at least part of it, you can barely hear yourself think.

Now a person might ask, "How is all this Amalek? Why isn't it just the natural course of history with pluses and minuses? Why call it Amalekian?"

Because Amalek is a spirit more than a people. Remember Balak and Bilaam, and how they tried to destroy the Jewish people? The Zohar says that their souls came from the level of Amalek in the spiritual realm. It is what fueled them in their efforts, and why combining their names results in the four letters of Amalek's name.[7]

There are only TWO directions in life: toward God and away from Him. There is no neutral ground, so at any given moment people are moving in one of the two directions. If something is even remotely part of Torah, it will help them move towards God. If something is not Torah-

---

[7] Zohar, Balak 194a.

based, it will draw them away from Him.

"Amalek" is the name of that spiritual reality with which non-spiritual realities are imbued. This world was created holy, and man is meant to do everything he can to restore it to that ultimate state. Amalek includes all the resistance to any such efforts, and can come in any form or size.

Even in levels of religious observance. Amalek doesn't mind making trade-offs, giving people some of what they want in order to get some of what he wants. Many observant people, seemingly acting in the name of God, have actually been the reason for the failure of certain efforts to further the cause of Creation.

That is why it is so important to "know thine enemy." On the final day of judgment, the truth about everything will be known. The veil will be long gone, and therefore Amalek will be gone as well. That is when we will be able to see every single time that Amalek, in some way or in some form, got our attention, stealing it away from where it rightfully belonged.

"THAT WAS AMALEK? THAT DISTRACTION came from Amalek? THAT SINGLE MOMENT I looked away, or my mind drifted, or I was emotionally distracted WAS AN ATTACK FROM AMALEK?"

Yes. If not in person, then in spirit. He went

after our da'as, our intellectual understanding, to confuse us about right and wrong. He wanted to make certain that we would act the way he prefers and become foot soldiers in his army. Millions of people around the world are fighting on behalf of Amalek, and they have no idea that they are, but rather think that they're just doing their own thing.

If he can't accomplish what he wants because we already know too much to fall prey to his antics, then he works instead on sabotaging our efforts to improve ourself and the world, on whatever level he can. That's when distraction becomes one of his most effective weapons, and we would have a difficult time believing how many times we have fumbled important spiritual opportunities because at a crucial moment, we weren't all there.

Therefore when we fight off emotional distraction while learning Torah or performing a mitzvah, we battle Amalek and win. Not the war, because THAT goes on until we leave this world or history comes to an end and Yemos HaMoshiach begins. But certainly a battle, and after enough such victories we find ourself more in control of our life and far more spiritually productive.

where are my emotions now

two
free will

ONE OF THE most discussed topics is surely free will. Do we have it? Do we NOT have it? What is it exactly? How does it work? The amazing thing is that, after thousands of years of discussing it, it is still so widely misunderstood, including by people who claim to be "experts" on the topic, both secular AND religious.

One thing is for certain. Something we can't afford to take for granted we take the MOST for granted. People just get up in the morning and go about their day, assuming that not only do they HAVE free will, but that they use it all day long. SHOCK will be their reaction when they find out how few times they actually did use it throughout the course of their ENTIRE life.

Earlier generations may have used free will more because they had no CHOICE but to use it. They grew up in poverty. They lived in fear for their life. Daily life for such people WAS a free-will choice.

For many born into a higher economic position, as has been the case for the last few generations, it has been a different story. Life ceased to be the best educator about free will because many of its challenges disappeared. Not for everyone, but for many people.

But nothing replaced the education gained from life experience, except perhaps the mistaken assumption that using free will is the most NATURAL thing in the world. People are born with the right to use free will, so why shouldn't they be born with the ability to use it?

"Hi. I'd like to drive a car."
"No problem. Have you driven before?"
"No, but it looks easy. I'm sure I can pick up what I need to learn as I go along."

Ludicrous, right? Driving is too complicated and far too dangerous to start on your own without prior knowledge or experience. Even WITH the knowledge and experience people remain bad drivers. How much more so WITHOUT it!

You can get through life without a car, especially if you live in a developed area. You can't get through life without free will, and more than likely you will NOT pick it up as you go along. Most people don't, but instead go to their graves thinking they made TONS of free-will choices when in fact, after all is said and done, they probably made very FEW.

Isn't it ironic that the more automated our life becomes, the more psychologically handicapped we seem to be? Once upon a time it was a given that an illness did what it wanted, forcing an unwell person to cope with it, to work with it. There wasn't much of a choice for anything else.

Now we have treatments for illnesses. We have ways to nurse ourself, and in many cases to also avoid suffering. People can live a long time without any serious illness, which is fantastic and something for which to be very grateful. It can lead to years of incredible productivity, both physical and spiritual. But it can also lead to a life of reduced exercise of free will, along with a crippled ability to use it.

The rabbis have told us:

This is the way of the Torah: Bread and salt

you will eat, measured water you will drink, on the ground you will sleep, a life of suffering you will live, and in the Torah you will labor. If you do this, "You are fortunate and it is good for you" (Tehillim 128:2). "You are fortunate" in this world, "and it is good for you" in the World to Come. (Pirkei Avos 6:4)

They have also said:

...be careful [not to neglect] the children of the poor, for from them Torah comes out. (Nedarim 81a)

What is the message? It's obvious. When it comes to MATERIAL pleasures, we do not require encouragement. The body often trips over itself trying to get what it wants, what makes it feel good. It's remarkable just how much pain people are prepared to endure NATURALLY for physical pleasure. Absolutely remarkable.

Not so when it comes to SPIRITUAL goals. The loftier the spiritual goal, the more coaxing the body needs to encourage it to go after it, not only to make the initial effort but certainly to sustain it once it begins to be a strain. It takes WILL, lots and lots of WILL.

The proof? The yaiush. When it comes to

material accomplishments, yaiush is rarely an option. People DIE trying to accomplish the impossible, with the hope that somehow they will overcome their limitations and the odds and win anyhow, or go down having tried.

Spiritual goals, unless they are turned into material goals (e.g., I will become a great talmid chacham so that people will honor me), require a lot of resolve to achieve. If this is true when a person chooses the spiritual goal himself, how much more so must it be true if the goal is thrown at the person, like unwanted illness or difficulty.

This is not just a RELIGIOUS issue. It is a HUMAN issue. This is why even the secular world has phrases such as "When the going gets tough, the tough get going" and "Mind over matter." They say that life is not always easy, and there are times when willpower is the ONLY thing that can enable someone to succeed when succeeding is not at all natural.

The bottom line is that free will, or at least the use of it, is not a given. It is only a potential, like bench pressing 250 pounds. If you don't learn how to bench press properly and build up your physical and psychological ability to do so, it's never going to happen. Similarly, if you don't learn how to properly use free will and build up your ability to do so, it's just not going to happen by itself.

In fact, what does free will even mean? What is will, and what is it supposed to be free of? Does using free will mean doing whatever I FEEL like doing, or does it mean doing what I WANT to do? These are not always the same, evidenced by the creation of something insidious called...diabolic sounding music is heard now...the snooze button.

Getting out of bed in the morning is not AL-WAYS the easiest thing to do. In fact, for some people, it NEVER is, but it's rather the END result of several presses on the snooze button, until guilt and fear of being late, together with a pinch of evaporating self-respect, overcome the inertia keeping the person in bed.

The obvious question is why people set their alarm at night for 6:45 the next morning if they didn't want to get up at that time. The obvious answer is that when the alarm was set, they had WANTED to get up at 6:45 a.m. It's just that when the alarm went off on time, they didn't FEEL like getting up then, or five minutes later, or five minutes after that.

What changed while they slept?

Well, when they set the alarm the night before, their body had yet to fall asleep and become cozy under the blankets. At that time their body was only getting ready to go to bed, which is what it felt like doing, so there was no need for it to rebel in any way. The plan to get up at 6:45 the next morning, at that time, was only a bridge to cross later.

Then the person went to sleep. During the many hours of sleep the body slipped into a state of complete relaxation and rest, kind of a blissful state of existence. It was time to stop doing things, to stop caring about anything or anyone, and just check out of life for the time being.

Then came the morning, and the alarm with it. The alarm said, "The fun is over. Time to get back into life again, to move around and do things, to meet responsibility and care about everything all over again." Even a person looking forward to the upcoming day has to overcome some bodily resistance to jump out of bed and kick-start his or her life again. We may WANT to get out of bed on time, but we don't necessarily FEEL like doing it.

If the goal is merely to get out of bed on time in the morning, then why fight it? Most things that go wrong from sleeping in can be rectified in one way or another. You can call in late. You can doven at a later minyan. You can apologize profusely to the person you stood up and make excuses. They'll be SOME regret, but it will be minimal.

But if the goal is something loftier, MUCH loftier, then getting out of bed on time in the morning is also a metaphor for ongoing life struggle. Feelings are strong and they dominate much of our life. But their most important contribution is when they run contrary to what we WANT to do, NEED to do—build a psychological stage that brings free will to life.

That's the "free" part of free will. It is choice that is free of those things in life that try to hold us back from doing what is most meaningful in life. It is the ability to do what we WANT to do when it flies in the face of what we FEEL like doing.

What ARE we supposed to WANT to do?

It's really quite straightforward, summed up by the following statement:

> This world is like a corridor before the World-to-Come. Rectify yourself in the corridor in order to be able to enter the banquet hall. (Pirkei Avos 4:16)

This analogy has never been more accurate and appropriate than today. Once upon a time Jews were so poor that they had to make weddings on Friday so that the Shabbos meal could double as the wedding meal. And even then it probably didn't come close to the average Shabbos seudah of today.

Today many families make TWO meals for each chasunah, the pre-meal, or smorgasbord for the guests lounging around in advance of the chupah, and the main sit-down meal after the chupah. In some cases, the food served BEFORE the chupah exceeds what more modest weddings serve as their main feast!

At some of these more extravagant weddings, it is possible to have a complete seudah before the chasunah. A little of this and a little of that adds up to a lot in the end, and with too little time to digest all of it before the main course is served, people often let entire plates of expensive food spoil, wasting money that might have otherwise gone to feed people who have no idea where THEIR next meal is coming from.

Not only that, but since good food is part of the fun of coming to a wedding, many people feel that they have gotten all the fun they came for after the smorgasbord and chupah. They never make it to the banquet hall, and it is not uncommon to see partially filled tables at a wedding seudah. Although many people had been there for the smorgasbord and chupah, they miss out on the main course.

Life isn't all that different. This can be a VERY enjoyable world, more so today than ever before. And whereas once being religious often interfered with material satiation, because it was a choice of one or the other, today we can literally have our religious cake and eat it too.

And eat it and eat it and eat it. So much of what was once considered to be a gentile way of life can now be incorporated into a Torah way of life as well. Comforts once considered to be antithetical to a Torah lifestyle went from being "bad" to "not so bad" to "okay" to "must have," and with it, the Olam HaZeh[1] MENTALITY that created and sustains such a lifestyle. We have been invited to the smorgasbord, and we're filling up.

The most fundamental rule about life is that this world is only meant to be a stepping stone to the next, the corridor to THE banquet hall of banquet halls, Olam HaBa—the World-to-Come. But unlike earthly weddings for which you only need to know the people getting married to be invited, you have PURCHASE your invitation to Olam HaBa, the World-to-Come.

With what currency?

With mesiras Nefesh—self-sacrifice.

The currency of the World-to-Come is self-

---

[1] This world.

sacrifice. Not just ANY self-sacrifice, but mesiras Nefesh for what counts most to GOD, which He has detailed in His Torah. The price of admission to the world of ULTIMATE pleasure—a small amount of which the rabbis have already told us gives far more joy than a lifetime of earthly pleasure[2]—is mesiras Nefesh to be good, TORAH good.

This means only one thing: FREE will choices, or choices that are FREE of the yetzer hara. If the yetzer hara is not fighting AGAINST a choice, then it is in FAVOR of it. That usually means it's a COMFORTABLE choice—and not only do comfortable choices not require much mesiras Nefesh, they certainly do not earn much in the World-to-Come.

Yes, doing a mitzvah counts for a tremendous amount, and doing it with the right intentions counts for even more. But doing it with mesiras Nefesh is like hitting the jackpot, and reaps rewards far beyond what a person might think while in this world. It's like saving a butterfly and being treated as if you saved the ENTIRE world.

This is the greatest secret of life. We know that mesiras Nefesh is important. We know that it is valued by God. But if people only understood to what extent this was really true, they would

---

[2] Pirkei Avos 4:22.

spend all their waking hours just looking for opportunities to do something with mesiras Nefesh.

This is only the FIRST part of the free-will discussion.

where are my emotions now

three
objectively speaking

MARKETING AND ADVERTISING are multi-billion dollar industries, and for an obvious reason: they work. How many people go shopping and purchase a specific brand simply because they saw it advertised? The product might be worth it, but it sold because it got into people's minds.

If people only knew how many times a day they make decisions that are influenced by unknown "others"! The best manipulators even give people the impression that their decisions are their own, free from outside influence. This is true when it comes to marketing products, and it is

ESPECIALLY true when it comes to marketing government policy.

The question is to what extent free will stops being FREE when it is influenced by outside factors, particularly when we don't even know about them. More importantly, how can we possibly know when we are being manipulated?

Objective standard.

Objective standards are used a lot—when school tests are graded, when business decisions are made, and for just about anything else people invest in. We acknowledge that in order to know if we are making a good decision about something important to us, we need an objective standard against which to compare it. It lessens the need for having to learn how to do something right from our OWN experience of having previously done something wrong.

Most of us WANT to do things the RIGHT way. We don't always FEEL like it, but we certainly WANT to. When we are most OBJECTIVE, we know this and try hard to live this way. When we are not, we tend to forget it and get sloppy with life.

Most of the time people don't have to think about it, because they are accustomed to living with a huge margin of error. As long as the crises remain within a certain range of manageability,

they feel little or no need to make course correc-
tions. It's only when people suffer beyond what
they bargained for that they are inclined to take a
long, hard look at their own life, and life in gener-
al.

Religious people are just as human as secular people, and therefore subject to similar ten-
dencies. They've already made major concessions
to God by living an observant life, and might
therefore assume that it's all God wants from
them until life makes them wonder otherwise.

They can, and often do, make the mistake of
assuming that the mitzvos they do guarantee a
life of free-will choices. But clearly humans can
adapt to different ways of life, even demanding
ones, until they live without much thought about
what they are really doing. Spiritual stagnation is
a problem for everyone, regardless of spiritual
level.

For people who do not believe in an OBJEC-
TIVE TRUTH, the discussion ends here. They are
doomed to learn what is right or wrong from life
lessons only, and life can be a VERY harsh teacher.
Countless people have lost innumerable things—
physically, spiritually, and both—from being
wrong.

This was essentially the very first choice
man had to make. There were two trees in the

middle of the Garden, Aitz Chaim—Tree of Life—and Aitz HaDa'as Tov v'Ra—Tree of Knowledge of Good and Evil. Although at first the Torah doesn't discuss the consequence of eating from the Tree of Life, it does mention the result of eating from the Tree of Knowledge: death.

Anyone unsure of how things turned out just needs to look around. Life is clearly not paradise. We make the best of it, and it has its moments, but paradise it is not. The Garden of Eden still exists, but not for us—not until history has played out and with it the necessity of choosing right from wrong. Even then entry will be by invitation only.

The Torah doesn't say what the Aitz Chaim actually is, or how one could learn from it. But Kabbalah does, and it is no coincidence that Torah is called the same thing as Aitz Chaim:

> It is a tree of life for those who grasp it. (Mishlei 3:18)

The big question is why ANYONE would choose to learn from a "tree" associated with DEATH when he or she could learn from one that is clearly associated with LIFE? No one would, or did, until the snake, a.k.a. the yetzer hara, entered the discussion and made the first marketing pitch of history:

> The snake said to the woman, "You will surely not die. For God knows that, on the day that you eat from it, your eyes will be opened and you will be like angels, knowing good and evil." (Bereishis 3:4-5)

SOLD! Chava bought the words of the snake, as the Torah tells us:

> The woman saw that the tree was good for food and that it was a delight to the eyes, and the tree was desirable to make one wise. So she took of its fruit, and she ate… (Bereishis 3:6)

And like EVERY successful marketing campaign, the word of mouth of one buyer results in the sale to another:

> And she gave also to her husband with her, and he ate. (Bereishis 3:6)

Had Adam and Chava WANTED to eat from the Aitz HaDa'as v'Ra? No! Did they FEEL like eating from it after the influence and manipulation of the snake? Clearly, yes. Did they live to regret confusing WANT and FEEL? Yes, for the rest of their life, as we too often do for the rest of our long and often sorry history.

We were expelled from the Garden and barred from the Tree of Life. But not forever. We can't go back to the Garden yet, but we can access the Aitz Chaim, not the actual tree itself—if that's what it really was—but in the form of Torah. And although a flaming sword may not guard this version of the Tree of Life, access is nonetheless granted only to the worthy.

While countless people debate whether Torah is really from God, or whether an objective truth really exists, those who know better use Torah as the standard by which to measure their decisions in life. If Torah sanctions it, the decision is on the right track. If not, a course correction is needed.

So as the clock ticks away on a meaningful life for disbelievers, some people, who believe that Torah is what it says it is, use Torah to maximize every waking moment. They get up in the morning, knowing how best to use their short time here on earth. When they go to bed, they know that they again contributed to their eternal "pension" plan. Or pray that should be the case.

Unfortunately, it is not just Torah plus mitzvos that equal the World-to-Come. True, a minimal amount of intention when learning Torah or doing mitzvos goes a long way in the Eternal World, but not nearly as far as we'll want it to have gone once we actually get there.

When we get to our own place in Olam HaBa, and watch others zooming past us to higher levels, we'll wonder what they did that we didn't. It won't have been due to their extraordinary wealth or almost superhuman abilities, because Heaven doesn't compare apples and oranges.

No, those people who surpass us were probably different in the one thing we all share alike—mesiras Nefesh. We can all be self-sacrificing for Torah learning or for the performance of mitzvos. We don't have do anything at the same level as anyone else, but rather each and every one of us has to do it to the best of our own ability.

That's the question we need to ask ourself when we wake up in the morning and when we go to bed at night: "Am I doing my PERSONAL best at the things that count most according to Torah?" The answer can rarely ever be "yes" if we just go through the motions, doing the will of God without our own will behind it.

When it comes to the will of God, it's not only about being mitzvah compliant. It's HIS will that we use OUR will at every opportunity we can. The more WE will in His service, the more impressed HE is with us. He gave us the Torah not just to tell us what to do, but to challenge us to sacrifice for it.

Sometimes in history that has resulted in the ULTIMATE sacrifice, DYING al kiddush Hashem, dying to sanctify the name of God. Most of the time it "only" means LIVING al kiddush Hashem, on the highest spiritual level we can, and that means moving beyond perfunctory observance.

We know this level exists and we tend to admire it in others. We read story after story about someone who lived his entire life this way, and we feel comfortable knowing that we could never do what he did. People like him were special but we're only mundane. God knows and understands this.

Perhaps. But it is more likely that we are selling ourself short, and in many cases, VERY short. People are inclined to confuse the yetzer hara's desire to FEEL comfortable with an inability to push themselves to overcome adversity and make an authentic free-will choice. They don't mind what they think are only harmless and innocent distractions, unaware of how tricky, subtle, and magical Amalek can be when it comes to getting us to look in HIS direction instead of GOD'S.

When it comes to food, we can pretty much see how our decisions affect us. Lots of foods taste amazingly good, but often for a not-so-healthy reason. We know from experience and have also been told that our body can handle a certain amount of unhealthy food and not miss a beat, literally.

But we also know that if we eat too much of such food, we'll get sick, or fat, or have a heart attack down the road. We can eat it at night and the next morning see the impact on the scale, or just not feel good until everything has been digested and our body has recovered from the assault.

If only bad decisions, or a lack of making them, could be completely obvious to us! That would make it so much easier to live a higher quality of life and to know better how to deal with diversity. The biofeedback would allow us to know where we are weak-willed so we could design an "exercise" program to strengthen ourself.

That is essentially what Torah does for us. It's the objective "person" in the room, the one who sees what we're doing and can tell how on or off we truly are. But it won't speak up unless we invite its criticism, which we do by looking into it in order to better understand what God REALLY wants from us, and how best to achieve it.

That's when we find out just how brilliant an objective voice it really is, and why we should rely on it more often to evaluate our level of choice. Then we can see just how free our will really is.

where are my emotions now

four

lesson from the past

IT'S SCARY TO think about how easily people can be persuaded to do stupid things. It happens a lot, even to people who seem too smart for such mistakes. As the Talmud says, "A person only sins when a spirit of insanity enters him."[1] This certainly makes for a LOT of "insane" people throughout history.

One episode that should have us scratching our head is that of the Meraglim.[2] Sent to spy out Eretz Yisroel, they ended up returning with an evil report, thus dooming the Jewish people to thou-

---

[1] Sotah 3a.
[2] Bamidbar 13:1.

sands of years of history. The ten spies themselves died horrible deaths, those who regretted believing the spies died in a battle they were told not to wage, and the rest of the guilty died during the next 39 years after digging their own graves and lying down in them.

What were the people thinking? It wasn't like today when people can argue about whether an obligation to make aliyah still exists. God was right there, and they knew it. He was actively and overtly involved in all their affairs. He made it clear that the purpose of leaving Egypt was to go to Eretz Yisroel. And they STILL rejected it? Were they suicidal?

Here's the BEST part. After they rejected the land and threatened to murder Yehoshua and Caleiv for going against them, God stepped in and lowered the boom, BIG time. He told everyone how HE viewed the situation, and pronounced their punishment, at which time they turned 180° on the spot. Were they surprised? No. They were SHOCKED by God's harsh reaction, and that was that.

And here we are, over 3300 years later, still paying the price of their grave error, still limping through history. Although many think we have moved on since that time, they are wrong. Or even worse, they are continuing on with the insanity of the spies. Today, more than ever, there are very important lessons to be learned from what they did, not just about Eretz Yisroel but about free will itself.

What really happened back then? On one side, there were 10 spies telling the nation that it was a mistake to go to Eretz Yisroel, because they would fail if they tried. On the other hand, there were Yehoshua and Caleiv painting a far rosier picture and trying to convince the nation that the question was not IF to go up, but rather HOW to go up.

What was the fundamental difference in these outlooks? Were the spies just being pragmatic, and Yehoshua and Caleiv just being overzealous youths? Or were they the ones being pragmatic, while the 10 spies, with the rest of the people they dragged to their side, were missing the entire point?

The Torah of course answers THAT question. Then what point did everyone, except a handful of party faithfuls, miss so badly? It's the same point that billions of people have missed over the ages, that when "the going gets tough, the tough get going." Making aliyah is supposed to be a free-will choice, not something we do because it is EASY to do. This is similar to the acquisition of Torah and the World-to-Come:

Three wonderful gifts were given by the Holy One, blessed is He, to the Jewish people, and all of them were given through suffering. They are Torah, Eretz Yisroel, and The World-to-Come. (Brochos 5a)

There seems to be an internal contradiction here. A gift is usually called that because it brings pleasure, not suffering. Few people ever give a gift of suffering, and even fewer people accept one. Unless, that is, the recipient realizes that the suffering itself IS a gift.

There is this also:

If a man says to you, "I have labored and not found," do not believe him. If he says, "I have not labored but still have found," do not believe him. If he says, "I have labored and found," you can believe him. This is true with respect to words of Torah… (Megillah 6b)

Are we saying that there have never been natural geniuses who have been able to learn quickly and effortlessly and accumulate a lot of Torah? Yes, but that's not the point. Genius is an asset for sure, but only with the proper attitude. The Jewish people have had plenty of geniuses over the millennia, but the ones who have made the greatest difference are the ones who knew how to be moser Nefesh[3] for Torah.

Why does it make a difference? The Talmud answers that question here:

> All is in the hands of Heaven except fear of Heaven, as it says, "Now, Israel, what does God, your God, ask of you? Only to fear Him…" (Devarim 10:12)…Rebi Chanina said in the name of Rebi Shimon bar Yochai: the Holy One, blessed is He, only has fear of God in His storehouse, as it says, "Fear of God is His treasure" (Yeshayahu 33:6). (Brochos 33b)

The topic of fear of God is almost as vast as it is important. On the simplest level, it means that we should take God and His mitzvos seriously. On a deeper level, it means that we should try to SEE Him in EVERYTHING and at ALL times. On a deeper level yet, it means that we should try to make a close relationship with God the most important thing in our life.

How? By climbing mountains for Him. Why does that work? Because the VALUE of something

---

[3] Self-sacrificing.

to a person is measured by what he or she is willing to PAY FOR IT.

Loose change?

No big deal.

Hard-earned money?

Impressive.

Your life?

Awesome.

Giving up one's life does not have to mean actual physical death, and it is not the ULTIMATE payment to God. On the contrary, death is a one-time occurrence, and many people have risen to the occasion for THAT. We are not sheep raised for slaughter, which is why God only demands our life in certain extenuating circumstances.

Giving up your life means making Torah priorities YOUR personal priorities. It means working on making Torah values the most valuable to YOU, so that you will have no problem extending yourself to living by them. That is the only reason, Rebi Shimon bar Yochai teaches us, that we are here.

And here's the essential point: Eternal pleasure, the ultimate goal, is built from every aspect of our mesiras Nefesh throughout our many lifetimes. Each time we reincarnate, we accumulate additional reward in the World-to-Come from each act of mesiras Nefesh.[4]

So when we lie down in bed at night and consider the kind of day we had, we need to ask only one question: How much mesiras Nefesh DID I use compared to how much I COULD have used? The more the two are alike, the better the day we will have had.

During wartime, some soldiers tend to stand out more than others. They even have medals of valor for such people, who went "above and beyond" the call of duty. Duty only required so much of them, but they expected more from themselves, and that impresses us.

What if people accidentally do something heroic? If they knew beforehand what they would be getting into, they would NEVER have done it. But they didn't. Instead, after finding themselves in a certain dangerous predicament, they had NO CHOICE but to do something that LOOKED heroic.

In many societies they might still get the medal. But if they are honest with themselves, they will feel underserving. Heroism is not a measure of the success of a redeeming act, but rather the amount of will that was invested in it to make it successful. "According to the suffering is the re-

---

4 Sha'ar HaGilgulim, Introduction 24.

ward,"[5] not according to the success of the act.

This is the point that the generation of the Spies missed, and the reason that God became so angry with them. They were taken out of Mitzrayim and given Torah to activate their free will, and to get it into far better shape. When they opted out of aliyah, they made it clear that success mattered more than effort, and that revealed how poorly they understood the reality of bechirah— free will. Their situation was just a MEANS to exercise exactly that.

Yehoshua and Caleiv, and those who stood with them, understood all this. They focused less on what it would take to conquer Canaan than on the free-will opportunity that doing so would afford them. They saw it for the climax that leaving Egypt was meant to be.

If so, this offers another spin on the verse:

> I am God, your God, Who took you out of the land of Egypt, to give you the land of Canaan, to be a God to you. (Vayikra 25:38)

On the surface, this verse means what the Talmud says, that we cannot relate to God the way we need to in the Diaspora. Only Eretz Yisroel

---

5 Pirkei Avos 5:23.

is the place for that.[6] As it says in Tuv HaAretz,[7] the border of Eretz Yisroel mirrors the opening to Heaven, so you can't get much closer to Heaven from down here than THAT.

On a free-will level, it means that Eretz Yisroel is the place we get to CHOOSE, and choosing is what brings us closer to God. After all, if the purpose of life is eternal union with God—and that is a function of our free-will choices—then those choices must be what God cherishes most about us, at least the meaningful choices.

Here's the point. Before we absorbed the yetzer hara into ourself, we weren't into comfort so much. Pleasure, yes—comfort, no. We understood that being created in the image of God meant using free will to the best of our ability, and any struggle involved in the process was well worth the result.

Then we made a miscalculation, sinned, and absorbed the yetzer hara into us. We literally became more physical, and therefore, more oriented toward physical comfort. There have always been a handful of righteous people who understood

---

[6] Kesuvos 110b.

[7] Written by Rabbi Noson Shapira in 1655. Rabbi Shapira came to Eretz Yisroel from Poland, learned with two of the greatest kabbalists of his time, and had access to many manuscripts of the Arizal, Rabbi Yitzchak Luria (1534-72).

what life was really about, and who did their best to achieve that goal. But the vast majority of people made physical comfort the goal, which always means avoiding pain whenever possible.

God gave us the Torah to teach us otherwise, and to provide a path to fulfillment, SPIRITUAL fulfillment. It wasn't meant for ALL mankind, just for the Jewish people and anyone else who wanted to join us. Once upon a time, maximizing free-will opportunity was a HUMAN thing. Thanks to the yetzer hara, it became mostly a JEWISH thing.

The yetzer hara took over mankind so much that people lost touch with the idea of free will. Torah provides the Jewish people with an antidote to the yetzer hara, enabling us to reclaim our free will.

When we lived in "Goshen,"[8] we kept to ourselves and followed the Torah's approach to life. When we moved out and into the non-Torah world, it was hard not to be VERY influenced by the comfort-seeking world around us, especially

---

[8] This is the area in which the family of Ya'akov first settled when they went down to Egypt, the idea being to live apart from the rest of Egyptian society and not be influenced by it. Once we started to move out of Goshen, we lost that spiritual protection. "Goshen" is therefore a metaphor for any time Jews live separately from the world around them, allowing them to pursue the ways of Torah.

as it increased and became more affordable.

We might think that if we are religious, we're impervious to such material effects, and are guaranteed to get our priorities straight. History shows otherwise, and the consequences have been widespread and debilitating. Like the spies, we look for the easy way out to serve God.

It doesn't work. It didn't work for the spies and it won't work for us. Free-will choice is the priority, and the more it is free of the yetzer hara, whose sole goal is physical comfort—ESPECIALLY at the cost of spiritual greatness—the more it gets our Creator's attention. And there is NOTHING more fulfilling or beneficial than THIS.

where are my emotions now

five

inside information

"DON'T BOTHER ME!"

"What do you MEAN, 'Don't bother me?'"

"Exactly what I said, DON'T...BOTHER...ME!"

"How can you even SAY that, especially on a day like today!"

"How can I NOT say it on a day like today?"

"You're going to make us miss EVERYTHING!"

"Do I have a choice?"

"I'd like to believe you do."

"Well, it's been nine months so far," Joy said, "and I have NOT yet found a way out."

Intellect thought for a minute, and then said, "I know, I know. I've been working on a solution day and night...It'll come, it'll come."

"You sound like a broken record," Joy said, sarcasm and hopelessness in his voice.

"I'm sure," Intellect said. "But, you have to believe it...I have to believe it, because the day we stop, well...what else will we have to live for?"

"But what if we DON'T find our way out?" Fear spoke up now, after listening quietly until that moment. "What if we're doomed to spend the rest of our life like this?"

Worry just stood there, nodding in agreement. The creases in his forehead revealed anxiety, and no nails remained to bite.

"I can't even remember the last time I smiled," Sadness said. "Even when the sun shines, the day feels really gray."

"Well," Joy complained, "how do you think I feel? You're used to being sad. For me, it's a REALLLL downer."

"Can't you just get your act together for an hour or two?" Intellect asked. "Moments like this don't come around everyday you know."

"No can do," Joy said.

"You're just being stubborn!" Impatience weighed in.

Joy looked long and hard at him, and finally said, "STUBBORN? STUBBORN! You think this is about being STUBBORN?"

"Yes!" Impatience said, standing his ground.

"Let me tell you something," Joy said, winding up. "This is the wedding of my own son! I've looked forward to this day for some time now already, and you think I don't care if I miss it?"

"Then why can't you just focus on something other than yourself for a while?" Intellect asked.

"How," Fear answered for Joy, "when all you can imagine is never getting better?"

"That is all true," a new voice said, strong and sturdy.

"Wh-Who are you?" Fear asked.

"That's Wisdom." Intellect answered.

"Friend of yours?" Sadness asked.

"More like MENTOR of mine."

"Maybe of YOURS," Joy jumped in, "but not of MINE."

"Until now, perhaps not," Wisdom said. "But it's never too late to learn a little wisdom."

"As if THAT'S going to help at all!" Worry said.

"Would you like to find out?" Wisdom said calmly, undeterred.

"What can you possibly say that I don't already know?" Joy asked.

Wisdom just smiled. "How easy it is," he thought to himself, "to be convinced that we know all we need to know to solve our problems. Small wonder," he realized, "that people can feel so hopeless about their situation! How can you hope when you think about all the potential solutions that have come and gone, and none of them worked."

"Did you know," Wisdom asked, "that the Talmud says that every illness is under contract to God?"[1]

Everyone else looked at each other, surprised by such a statement.

"Under contract?" Joy asked.

"What kind of contract?" Worry seconded.

"Well, according to the Talmud, God sends illness to a specific person for a specific period of time, to be cured by such-and-such a person at such-and-such a time."

There was silence.

"Really?" Frustration, who tended to hang out with Impatience, spoke up for the first time. "Then what good does it do to try to get rid of it, if anyhow it may be meant to last for a longer period of time?"

"Yeah," agreed Worry. "Here we are, playing hit and miss with different remedies, and there's only ONE out there meant for us! I mean, what's the point in that?"

"That's a different part of the Talmud," Wisdom answered, and Intellect knew exactly where.

---

[1] Avodah Zarah 56a.

"Brochos…5a," Intellect chimed in.

"Good for you!" Wisdom congratulated him.

"It's where the rabbis discuss the whole of suffering," Intellect continued.

"Correct," Wisdom said, "among MANY other places in the Talmud and midrashim…"

"So what does it say," Joy asked, "if Tehillim tells us to serve God with joy?"[2]

"You're right, it does," agreed Wisdom, "and it's not a contradiction."

"I'm afraid it is," said Fear. "Pain and pleasure are opposites, so…"

"Really? They are?" asked Wisdom.

"Yeah, they are?" echoed Intellect.

"Sure," Fear insisted.

"Well, let me ask you a question. What's our greatest pleasure in life?"

"The greatest?" Joy asked, challenged by the question. "It's been so long since I've had it, I can't remember which one is the best!"

Intellect answered first.

"I'd say it's accomplishing meaningful things in life…using our potential for good things."

Wisdom looked around and asked, "Does everyone agree with Intellect?"

---

2 Tehillim 100:2.

The rest looked at each other, and finally one of them said, "I guess…"

"Okay, well let's say that it is, for argument's sake," Wisdom continued. "Does it ever cause you any SUFFERING when you work at completing something important to you?"

"Suffering?" Joy questioned. "I mean it's tiring, and stressful…but suffering? I don't know if that is suffering like this, per se."

"What's the difference?" Wisdom probed.

Joy thought for a long moment, and then finally answered. "For one, if I want to end that suffering, I just have to stop what I am doing…"

"And that doesn't hurt too?" Wisdom asked.

Joy thought some more.

"Yes, I suppose it does. But not THAT much."

"Okay," Wisdom concluded, "I guess we can all agree that pain and pleasure are NOT opposites, but often come because of one another. As they say, 'No pain, no gain!'"

"And according to the suffering is the reward!"[3] Intellect added.

"That's right."

"That may be true," Frustration stepped in, but this depression is, well, depressing, day after

---

[3] Pirkei Avos 5:23.

day after day. I mean, it sucks all the joy out of life."

"And all the life out of Joy!" Joy remarked sardonically.

"Sadly it does," Wisdom agreed. "The question is whether it really has to."

"It seems like it does." Frustration said.

"Yes," agreed Joy.

"To me as well," Fear concurred.

"Hmm," Wisdom said sympathetically, "I can see why you would say that."

"So we're right?"

"Not unless you want to be!"

They looked at each other, and Joy said, "I think it is safe to say that this is ONE time we would not mind being wrong!"

The rest of them nodded in agreement.

"Good," said Wisdom. "Then allow me to tell you a story."

"A story?" Joy asked.

"Yes, a story."

They all made themselves comfortable, curious to hear what Wisdom had to say.

"Once there was a young man who thought he knew exactly what he wanted from life, and what to put into it. For almost the first two decades of his life, he had never considered that he was meant for anything else, and he never let anything rock his boat."

"But," Wisdom continued, "life has a way of rocking our boat whether we like it or not."

"Tell me about it," Fear couldn't help but say.

"It's because WE don't run our lives, only ruin them," Wisdom explained.

"What do you mean by 'ruin them'?" Worry asked.

"Well, we think we know what's best for us," Wisdom said, "and often sell ourself short. We don't take the time to figure who we really are and how we are different from others. The great Shlomo HaMelech wisely told us that every child has his or her own path to follow in life.[4] Yet we rarely consider what our OWN path is, and we just go with the flow around us!"

No one said anything, but they realized it was true.

"Everyone has a unique soul, with unique traits, drives, and abilities. Life can never be 'one size fits all,' and when we act as if it does, we can easily put on the wrong size, which only leads to personal problems."

Wisdom was making good sense, and he had them thinking.

---

[4] Mishlei 22:6.

"Anyhow," he continued, "that's what happened to our hero. He was so busy listening to what he had THOUGHT was his destiny that he lost track of what it really was."

Wisdom looked at each one of them, to make sure they were all getting it. They seemed to be, so he went on.

"But our soul doesn't forget, and it doesn't forgive either. Going against its purpose in life…"

"Which is?" Frustration jumped in.

"Tikun, of course!" Intellect answered for Wisdom. "We're only HERE to rectify our soul. Everything else we do in life is just for this purpose."

"I don't know about that," said Joy. "There are LOTS of people out there just having a blast, and not one of them looks too concerned about rectifying his or her soul!"

"That's a proof something?" Intellect asked. "God destroyed the world through a flood because people missed the point of life. Look at world history, and all the death and destruction! Mankind has never really been with the program and has paid for it over the ages…and will REALLY pay for it in the next world!"

"That's right," Wisdom corroborated. "But that's not the point right now. The point now is that our soul knows what we're here to do, and

WE'RE here to help the person in which we find ourself to translate THAT into everyday LIFE."

"Anyhow," Wisdom continued, "this young man's soul got the better of him after a while, and forced him to take some time off to reconsider his path in life."

"Wow, that seems scary," Fear said, a quiver in his voice.

"Oh, it was scary all right," Wisdom agreed. "But not as scary as what was about to come up!"

Fear was frightened, and he hid behind the rest of the emotions.

"Tell us what followed," Impatience pleaded.

"Well, once he left the stream of society, he felt as if he had been left behind by all his friends. He didn't know what he wanted to do instead, so he also felt lost. The longer he was away from what everyone else was doing, the more this was true. A sense of failure set in, and then fear that life would pass him by."

"I don't know if I can handle much more of this!" Sadness said.

"Don't worry, don't worry," Wisdom assured him. "The story has a happy ending!"

For one brief moment, Joy felt a flicker of hope. It was fleeting, but that it occurred at all was promising, at least for a moment.

Wisdom continued.

"The situation went from bad to worse, forcing him to become extremely introspective. Not recognizing himself any more, he went in search of himself. He started with his childhood and worked his way to the present day. He dug up old pictures, and asked relatives for their memories of him and their impressions. At the same time, he researched psychology to better understand what he was going through, which by that time had become depression. He even questioned the value of continuing on in life if he couldn't enjoy it."

"I can relate," Sadness said sadly.

Joy put his arm around Sadness to console him, and for a split second, the change of focus was somewhat uplifting.

"He reached rock bottom and could find nothing good about himself. He was at a loss for what to do. Family couldn't help. Friends didn't help him. Even therapists offered him little to work with."

"What happened already?" Impatience blurted out. "I can't stand not knowing the solution!"

"Well, while he was walking home one fine summer day that he couldn't enjoy, he noticed something about himself...something he had not paid attention to before...something he felt confident was truly a part of him..."

"Yes...yes...?" Joy pushed.

"He noticed that…he never gave up."

"What?" said Frustration. "That's it? That's what he found out about himself? That was the BIG deal?"

"Oh, it was a big deal all right," Wisdom told him. "It was a big deal because it became his emotional turning point, back from the abyss of depression to a life happier and more productive than that of most other people, who never went through what he did."

Joy stepped closer. "Okay, I'm listening."

Wisdom smiled and said, "Good idea. Anyhow, finding that one good trait he clearly had—because he just refused to give up—provided a kind of psychological peg with which he could pull himself up."

"Did it work?" Joy asked.

"It took time, a LOT of time, but yes, it did work."

"I don't know…"

Everyone looked around to see where THAT voice came from.

"Who are you?" Sadness asked, "and why are you so…GRAY?"

"You have to ask? Obviously I'm Doubt."

"Ughhhhh!" Frustration blurted out. "And just when things were starting to look up!"

But Wisdom was unfazed. "Of course you don't know," he said. "This is new to ALL of you…"

"But…" Doubt started to say, and was immediately stopped.

"But nothing!" Wisdom said. "What difference does it make anyhow? What will you gain by living in doubt? You want to paralyze everyone and go nowhere just to stay safe? How is that safe? Isn't it better to go down trying than to go nowhere because you tried nothing?"

"But…" Doubt persisted.

"Enough of the buts!" Wisdom cut him off again, knowing that doing so would weaken him. "Learn a lesson from the person in the story. He put doubt aside and instead focused his energy on finding additional positive aspects of his life to lift his spirits."

"Where did he find the patience?" Impatience asked.

"Did he have a choice?" Wisdom pointed out. "He wanted to return to life, to be able to enjoy the enjoyable moments once again, and he was determined not to stop until he did."

"I'm afraid that won't work for us," Fear said.

"I'm sure you're afraid," Joy said. "It's your job. But it's my job to chase after you, and I'm willing to give it a shot!"

"Great stuff!" Intellect said, and then looked at Wisdom for more information.

"Yeah, great stuff." Wisdom repeated. "But first a spoiler alert."

"A spoiler WHAT?" someone asked.

"A spoiler ALERT..." Impatience said impatiently. "It means that he's going to spoil the ending for us by telling something in advance."

"Well, in this case," Wisdom explained, "I'm going to make it easier for you..."

"Please continue!" Joy urged.

"Heyyy, that's my job!" Impatience complained.

"What, you think you're the ONLY one who gets impatient around here?" Joy shot back.

"Hmm..." Impatience growled.

"People, people, people," Intellect cut in, returning the floor to Wisdom. "Let's stay focused!"

"Anyhow," Wisdom continued, "his plan was to do things that are so incredibly distracting, in a positive way, in order to divert his attention away from himself for a short while, just to feel something positive even if only for a few seconds. You see, he began to understand that the reason he couldn't enjoy happy moments was because his emotions just weren't there to enjoy them. Sunny days felt gray, he understood, because his emotions didn't see them, but instead felt what was not sunny."

"To make a long story short, this young man realized that if he were going to heal and become 'normal' again, he was going to have to bring his emotions back on line, to experience life as it was happening...the way he was seeing it. Fear, doubt, impatience, etc., caused his emotions to separate from his intellect. They became so obsessed with what they were going through that they were always some place other than he was at each moment."

"Like we are now," Joy said, rethinking the last year of life, "and like we have been this whole year!"

"That's right," agreed Wisdom. "If Intellect were to tell you what HE has been seeing and living, you'd think that he belonged to someone else! His version of reality over this past year is probably VERY different from yours!"

"Man, have we ever missed out!" Disappointment said.

"When did you get here?" Sadness asked.

"I've been here the whole time. Well, at least the last year. Before then, I used to come and go, and sometimes I didn't even come at all!"

"Those were the good old days," Joy reminisced.

"For YOU maybe!" Disappointment barked.

"Is there anything else?" Joy asked, eager to get started.

"You just have to know," Wisdom warned, "that it will look as if you are not succeeding at first. Bad habits are hard to break. Fears are difficult to put behind us. Disappointment is constant. Doubt..." Wisdom inhaled deeply, "is ALWAYS on the offensive."

Intellect looked at his battle scars. How many times had he gone to war against doubt, winning some battles and losing others...It hurt just to think about it.

"It's like building a building," Wisdom described. "You start with a big hole in the ground, then lay the foundation, and gradually you make your way out of the hole. At first it looks as if nothing major is being accomplished, and for a while, passersby even stop checking. And then one day, one GLORIOUS day, enough of the building takes shape to become recognizable as a building. Past that important turning point, it becomes more so with each passing day."

Wisdom paused to give them time to consider his words, and then brought his point home.

"We have a mission ahead of us," he said, sternly. "We need to put this guy back together again, so ALL of us can live life to its fullest and make good use of our time here on earth in preparation for the World-to-Come. Life is a war, and in war pain and suffering do not stop us from carrying out our mission. FUTURE happiness depends on it!"

"It's our job, and it always has been, to just try to be the very best US we can be. There will be good days and there will be bad days, good times and not-so-good times. We will get things and lose things, see our plans come to fruition or watch them blow up in our face!"

"Sheesh!" Fear said. "You don't have to be so dramatic!"

"Oh yes I do!" Wisdom corrected. "Life IS dramatic, and we are its main actors. We're the heroes, or at least we're supposed to be! We need to come together so that we can get our act together!"

"Wow," Sadness said, "you should be a motivational speaker!"

Wisdom smiled.

"And let's not forget one VERY important detail. It says that those who come to purify themselves, Heaven helps them. If someone sanctifies himself a little, Heaven will sanctify him a lot.[5] It means that if we just push ourself to do our part,

---

[5] Yoma 37b.

even just a teensy bit, we'll get the help from God that we need to succeed! So, whaddaya say?"

"I'm in!" Joy said enthusiastically.

"Me too!" said Sadness.

"I'm certainly in!" Frustration shouted.

One by one each gave the plan his seal of approval, until it was unanimous. Wisdom and Intellect looked at each other, clearly proud about the turn of events.

* * *

As Akiva sat there, searching for motivation for his next positive act, he suddenly felt a strange burst of enthusiasm, one he had not felt for, well, at LEAST a year. He didn't know why, but he felt as if he were getting better, and that life would improve.

It had taken a lot of time to get to this point, and it would take even more to go past it. But at least he knew he was finally heading in the direction he WANTED to go, and he actually FELT very good about it.

six
unification

where are my emotions now

UNIFICATION IS A universal concept, literally. It's as if the entire universe seeks unity, which it does, for a very fundamental reason. The universe came from unity and, as Kabbalah explains, it will eventually return to it. As commonplace as dissent has become, it is nonetheless disturbing and discomfiting, even though it is only a temporary reality.

"Hear O Israel, the Lord our God, the Lord is One." Jews have been saying this at least twice a day for thousands of years now. Its meaning is both obvious AND profound—it teaches us not only about the essential, fundamental unity of our Creator, but also about the essential, fundamental unity of Creation.

If it weren't for the yetzer hara, we would already have unity. Amalek and the yetzer hara are best buddies, and they're on the same spiritual team. So if Amalek's crime is that he divides God's name,[1] then it must be the goal of the yetzer hara as well. Together they tear our personal world apart, which tears the world itself apart.

Their weapons are many and dramatic, anything that might cause "machlokes"[2] on any level, anywhere and at any time. We have but one weapon against them—the most powerful of all—WILL. Only will is powerful enough to invoke the necessary help we need from Heaven to overcome the odds and achieve unification.[3]

Two examples make this point.

In many siddurim it says that one should begin morning prayers with the words, "I am prepared to fulfill the mitzvah of 'Love your neighbor as yourself.'" It was the great kabbalist Rabbi Yitzchak Luria who insisted that this declaration be inserted into our prayer books.

---

[1] Rashi, Shemos 17:16.
[2] Division.
[3] Kiddushin 30b.

Why place it HERE at the beginning? Un-questionably, it is an important mitzvah that we should be reminded of on a daily basis, but why right before tefillah? Why not at the end, like oth-er important mitzvos of which we are reminded?

Because it isn't at all uncommon for people to be bothered by others in a minyan. Not every-one does the same thing the same way. Some people take certain parts of the service more seri-ously than others. Others have idiosyncrasies that seem normal to them but somewhat weird to others. In short, it isn't hard to be critical of others when praying in a minyan.

And that's a big problem. The whole point of a minyan is synergy. Halachically,[4] just 10 people need to be praying together to make an official minyan.[5] Hashkofically,[6] those 10 people need to be on the same page, literally and metaphorically. That doesn't happen when someone is pushed away emotionally through criticism. When people are divided, the power of being unified is squan-dered, rendering prayers far less effective.[7]

---

[4] Legally.

[5] Certain parts of the service can only be said when 10 men pray together.

[6] Philosophically.

[7] Praying in a minyan adds a spiritual boost to each person's prayer, allowing it to ascend higher.

The yetzer hara is good at pointing out the flaws of others, as well as justifying the criticism. It also distracts us from the machlokes that results, and the personal loss it causes on many levels. It takes a STRONG act of will to ignore that, to CHOOSE to feel good about our fellow minyan members.

The other example has to do with a simple act of kindness. How many times has someone needed help, but the people in the vicinity pretended not to notice? How good can they feel about themselves, knowing they left a fellow human being in distress? RELIEVED, perhaps, but GOOD? Never.

Then there are the people who overcome their innate desire for physical relief, and they lend a helping hand. They CHOOSE not to be selfish, and are rewarded with the sincere appreciation of the person they helped. How good do they feel about themselves afterward? They feel GREAT!

If you gave one of those unselfish people a thousand dollars, with no strings attached, he or she would probably still not feel as good.

Excited, for sure.

Joyful, unquestionably.

Unified? Not really.

Why? Because money, however wonderful it is, can impact us for good only so much. Personal unification occurs when body and soul are working together, and the pleasure from that is UNBELIEVABLE. The only way money can achieve that is if it makes possible the performance of something godly, but even then it won't be the money that's really doing it, but rather the WILL to use the money in that particular way.

Being selfish is instinctive. It's the body doing its thing, the yetzer hara following ITS natural instinct. It takes an act of WILL, therefore, to be selfless. When it happens, soul and body line up, unify, and the growth and pleasure are not only tremendous, but eternal.

Eternal? Yes, eternal. It has to do with what metaphysically happens when body aligns with soul. It doesn't just result in a sense of personal wholeness, which in and of itself is a wonderful level to reach. It results in a portal to another dimension altogether.

It's kind of like a wormhole—a spiritual one. A physical wormhole is a theoretical passage through space-time that creates a shortcut for a long journey across the universe. It can be visualized as a tunnel with its two ends at separate points in space-time.[8]

When body and soul are unified—and only an eternally meaningful act can really do that—then it's as if a tunnel appears, providing a shortcut to a much higher spiritual dimension. We may not be able to travel up it, but its light and blessing can nonetheless flow down to us, imbuing our very being with a level of otherworldliness.

This is the deeper level of the meaning of Shabbos being one-sixtieth of the World-to-Come.[9] If a person observes Shabbos both in body AND spirit, then Shabbos itself acts as a portal as well to the eternal reality of Olam HaBa.[10] The TRUE pleasure of Shabbos is the taste of eternity that Shabbos provides for the person who "does" Shabbos properly.

It's something that an out-of-sync person can't really understand—how to align the body with the soul. How can someone understand the enormous pleasure people enjoy by doing so when he or she has never had such an experience?

---

[8] Wikipedia.
[9] Brochos 57b.
[10] The World-to-Come.

The rabbis teach:

One hour of pleasure in the World-to-Come is better than all the time in this world. (Pirkei Avos 4:17)

Someone who has not tasted such a level of pleasure would find it hard—no, impossible—to fathom. The material world has a lot of pleasure to offer, but not even the richest people in the world can enjoy all of it. And yet, compared to an hour of eternal pleasure, it's as if all those material pleasures didn't even exist!

How is that possible? We ask this question only because we are starting from the wrong side. We were not born into Paradise. We were not created in a world of ultimate pleasures. On the contrary, mankind was born and raised in exile, and pleasure is usually something we have to work hard for.

The same is true of spirituality. No one is religious from birth. Every child is born with the instinct to be selfish, and has to learn to use will in order to overcome that instinct. Spiritual growth and accomplishment are usually the result of effort and self-sacrifice.

But that's not the way man was originally made. He lived in Paradise from Day One of his existence. He was so spiritual that his skin was more like light than like our skin today.[11] The world to which he was exiled, that his descendants would come to love, was tasteless for him, as long as he had a memory of what he had once enjoyed.

He must have watched with anxiety how hard people had to work to feel even a tiny fraction of the pleasure he knew automatically in the Garden. It must have pained him to see how difficult it was to be spiritual in comparison to how natural it had been for him in Paradise. HE surely would have no trouble understanding the words of the mishnah about pleasure.

In short, prior to his sin, Adam HaRishon was in spiritual sync. His body was on the same team as his soul. They worked together, in tandem. It was the sin that separated their unity, shutting down the portal from the eternal world to the temporal via the soul to the body.

This is ultimately what distress causes, however it comes. Pain divides our emotions, pulling them away from the intellect. We have expressions such as "mind over matter" for this reason, to encourage people to resist the tendency to allow "matter" to overcome mind, eventually mak-

---

[11] Drushei Olam HaTohu, Drush Aitz HaDa'as, Siman 4.

ing a person fall apart and forego the challenge of life, at least temporarily.

This is why unhappy people not only emit a low level of energy, but they also tend to suck energy from others. When people are so out of sync with their soul that its energy, which comes from God, cannot make it into their body in any large amount, they become hungry for energy. Without enough of their own, they have to draw it from others.

It's just the opposite with respect to happy people. They seem to bubble over with energy, at least for the duration of their happiness, and THAT will depend on how eternal the source of their joy is. If it is material, it won't last long. If it is spiritual, it can last forever—which includes an entire lifetime.

Why? Because God is the Source of ALL energy, as we say in the Shema. We refer to Him as "One" because everything exists WITHIN Him. Something only exists because HE wills it, and then He sustains it with the necessary energy. If something has energy, then it is from God and only from God.

In a very real sense, when a person becomes unified, he or she unifies God as well, so to speak. Since we're a part of Him, if we're divided, that implies a division within some aspect of HIS reality. At least that is the way He makes it seem, for OUR benefit and the benefit of free will. Unify yourself and you unify the perceivable reality of God as well.

That's why it feels so good to be unified, to be shalaim—whole. It's not just personal completion we feel, but unification with the Divine, and contrary to what the physical tries to teach us, there is no greater pleasure. Tikun—personal rectification—is exactly this: lining up our personal reality so that we can line it up with God's.

That's what life is ALL about, and it clearly cannot be the easiest thing to do. It takes acts of will, and the greater the will expended, the more personally unified we can become, resulting in greater and more long-lasting pleasure.

where are my emotions now

seven
true rectification

TIKUN. RECTIFICATION. THIS is what life is ALL about. We don't reincarnate to have more fun, a thicker steak, a better wine, or a bigger house. We come back, and we come back, and we come back again if we have to, as many times as necessary, for one thing and ONE thing ONLY: personal rectification.

How do we know this? The truth is that it should be obvious from life itself. Sure, there are many ways to live irresponsibly and enjoy illicit pleasures. But time and time again we realize that we feel the most whole when we act maturely, responsible, charitably.

True, a debate rages over whether this is the result of nature or nurture, an inborn divine conscience, or social training. But if it is so against human nature, then why did the first guy instill it into society, and how did he get so many people to follow him?

It's possible to sidestep that argument because we can, as they say, cut to the chase. All that's necessary is to BELIEVE in God and His Torah, and ACCEPT His loyal followers, such as the Ari HaKodesh,[1] as authoritative,. We can turn to the very first page of the Arizal's "Sha'ar HaGilgulim," literally "Gate of Reincarnations," and read how EVERY gilgul we EVER live is for TIKUN and TIKUN only. End of discussion.

What IS tikun? That too is on the first page of Sha'ar HaGilgulim, and it continues over the next 200 pages. However, it can be summed up with a very short phrase: soul rectification. These two words, however, can only be explained with a LOT of detail and many historic examples—if we REALLY want to understand tikun and how to take command of it.

---

[1] Rabbi Yitzchak Luria (1534-72), one of the most authoritative kabbalists to have ever lived. His teachings are not considered to be mere opinion or interpretation, but actual fact, the result of Ruach HaKodesh, directly from divine sources, including from Eliyahu HaNavi.

Most people aren't particularly interested, at least as long as life is tolerable. When life goes as THEY plan, with only mild deviations, they're prepared to go with the flow. Even religious people, who believe in the eternal reward of the World-to-Come, seem content to assume that what they are already doing is basically good enough to make sure that they'll get to Olam HaBa, and that they won't have many regrets once they do.

It's as if we are taught:

"Here's Torah. It came from God, so live according to it as much as possible. Everything else will take care of itself."

That's like telling a game show contestant, "You only have to run from here to that finish line 50 feet away," and after she says, "Oh, well, that sounds easy enough," you add, "But you have to do it blindfolded, with one leg tied back, and you need to start off in the wrong direction." All of sudden the easy just became incredibly difficult.

Contrary to what it may look like, few people just breeze through life. And if they do, it is likely that they are not going to breeze into the World-to-Come. The opposite is true: you either pay now or pay later. It's a great merit to be able to pay NOW. It can be quite punishing to pay LATER.[2]

Sometimes it takes MANY gilgulim for people to finish just about everything they have to do. They may have only a little bit left, which God may decide they should take care of in this world rather than the next one. But a challenge may be required in order to complete the tikun, which sometimes means coming back in a way that makes performing even a small mitzvah difficult.

The point is that what WE see when we look at others never gets anywhere close to the entire story about them and their personal struggles. There is just no way to compare one person to another, and certainly not in a SINGLE lifetime. It's a story that only God knows and only He can judge. Anyone else who tries to do that is attempting to play God and is simply wasting his time.

We can't even compare ourself to those with whom we are the closest, or have known for the

---

[2] Hakdamos u'Sha'arim, Sha'ar 6, Ch. 9. It is possible, the Arizal explains, for some souls to have finished their own tikun and then return to this world solely to help others (Sha'ar HaGilgulim, Introduction 2). They've paid their dues in previous lifetimes, and really have no reason to be here, in this world, for themselves. Therefore they do not require any real challenges in life because they're working overtime, so to speak.

longest time—not even family members. What we see is NOT what we get, because the souls of others are invisible to us, as is everything they have gone through in this lifetime and previous ones. If we can't even know OURSELF well, then how can we possibly hope to know OTHERS well?

In a sense, we're in this world all alone. Stand on the most crowded corner in the world, and you're still basically by yourself. It's only you and God—everyone else around is just part of some dream that you can't control or even fully understand.

So where does that leave us? With our own life and our own personal tikun. No matter how trivial, sudden, or random a personal experience may seem, it was custom-designed by God, for US, for our own personal tikun...even if dozens of others seem to share the same experience. How it helps with their personal tikunim is up to THEM, not up to US.

Having said that, it would seem highly productive and prudent to sit down at various times and consider the question, "What am I here to fix?" If life shows us anything at all, it is that this is not a one-coffee question. It requires a lot of thought, a lot of introspection, and a lot of self-knowledge.

Furthermore, this is not a question that we can ask only once in our life. It is a question that we have to come back to countless times. Life isn't the only mystery that unfolds with time. We unfold too, and constant self-evaluation is crucial for making the most of our experience in history.

It is absolutely amazing how many people have come and gone without ever becoming aware of why. This is also problematic. God will allow some people to think that they live under the radar, and then He shows them otherwise, BIG TIME, in the next world. Others, however, He may believe in enough to shake them up now, to give them a chance to make good in their current gilgul, with or without their conscious consent. That can be VERY distressing.

Having said THAT, we're still left with the question about what personal tikun actually is. So without further ado, let's briefly go over the path a person is supposed to follow while walking the face of the earth.

The first thing to note is that we have five levels of soul.[3] It's ONE soul, but it has five levels, each one more spiritual than the one below it. All levels have to be rectified, ideally the first time we're here, but if not, then over the course of

---

[3] Sha'ar HaGilgulim, Introduction 1.

many reincarnations.

Fortunately we don't have to start from scratch each time. That would be pointless because we'd end up going nowhere spiritually. Basically, we pick up in each new life where we left off in the old one, making tikun cumulative.

The lowest level of soul—with which everyone begins and unfortunately many do not grow past—is called "Nefesh." It interfaces with the body in the blood, animating it but not really elevating it. Animals have this level of soul too, which is why someone who remains on the level of Nefesh can end up seeming more similar to an animal than to man.

People who grow spiritually will rectify whatever sub-level of Nefesh they are on at the time. If they grow spiritually enough, they will be able to move on to the next soul level , which is called "Ruach." By then they will be on a whole different spiritual level, with greater spiritual aspirations.

The level of Ruach also has sub-levels. People who grow from sub-level to sub-level can completely rectify the ENTIRE level of Ruach, and earn the opportunity to begin rectification of the next level up, which is called "Neshamah." This process sounds a LOT easier than it is, which is why so few people seem to do it these days.

It works the same way on the level of Neshamah, but by that point we're talking about levels of spiritual greatness that very few manage to achieve in our time. Beyond Neshamah are the levels of Chayah and Yechidah, which no one can reach at this stage of history, including the great Moshe Rabbeinu.

Tikun is all we're here to do. Scholastic achievement, making friends, creating a family, reaching Torah goals, making money...having fun... they are all a side show and, at best, a means to the far more noble end, Tikun. It's too bad that so many people see it the other way around.

People who enter a marathon with the goal to finish it do everything they can to achieve that end. If something happens to slow them down during the race, they fight against it in order to finish anyhow. They may have to hobble the final part in pain, and cross the finish line hours after everyone else has gone home, but they do it, no matter what, because that is their defining goal.

Some people are rich and some are poor, some are healthy and some are physically challenged. Some have a great family background and many friends, while others live in loneliness. This can make life either pleasant or unpleasant, but none of that changes what we're supposed to be doing while we are here. The body may complain and ask, "Why bother if life is so painful?" The soul answers back, "Because pain doesn't override the need for tikun, and in many cases only increases it."

This is the reason many people never leave the level of Nefesh. They're here to enjoy themselves, and see adversity as an obstacle to be eliminated or at least ignored. Spiritual growth is not a priority for them, and in many instances isn't even on their roadmap.

Happy is the person who understands the purpose of life and is ambitious enough to search for clues about how to live it. He or she will find the path, as it says, "Someone who comes to purify himself, they help him."[4] Not only will he be able to handle adversity, but he will use it to reach even greater spiritual heights, and in doing so, achieve personal completion, the only true source of joy in life.

---

4 Yoma 38b.

98❖WHERE ARE MY EMOTIONS NOW?

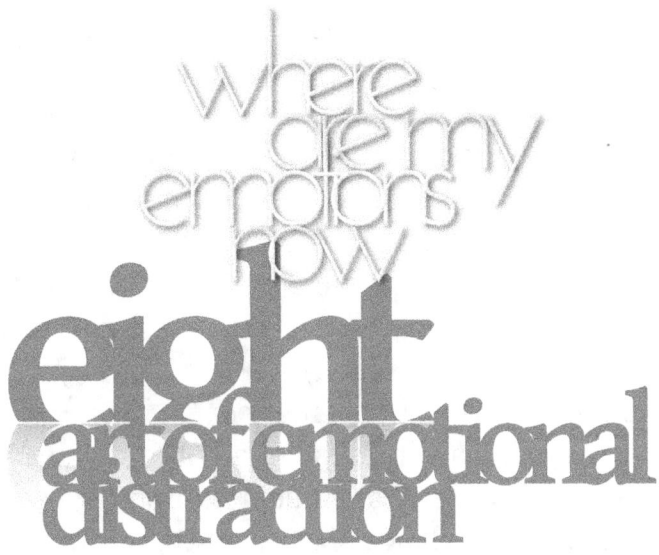

eight
where are my emotions now
art of emotional distraction

AMALEK'S WEAPON OF choice is emotional distraction. Physically killing a Jew only sends them directly to the World-to-Come. But distracting a Jew away from his or her personal tikun reduces their portion there. THAT is a victory for Amalek.

When it comes to materialistic distractions, they can be Amalekian-made. When it comes to other distractions, such a physical or psychological pain, he might or might not be the cause of it, at least directly. But he certainly knows how to use both to his "military" advantage, allowing whatever is bothering a person to distract them away from personal tikun.

So, why not FIGHT fire WITH fire? Why not learn from Amalek to our spiritual advantage?

How does this work?

War actually is a "good" example. War is life and death. In the heat of it, bombs fall close by while bullets whiz by. At any moment a person can be hit by either and be seriously injured or even killed. Even should a person survive, there is the fear that the enemy will win. There just isn't time to focus on trivial matters.

During a war, all other emotions take a back seat to the need to remain sharply focused on outliving the dangers. If a person, during peacetime, mentions they are depressed, others will send them to a psychologist. If a person mentions they are depressed while bombs are falling, they will seem overly self-focused and out of touch with reality.

The reason is obvious. During peacetime, death becomes less of a threat and therefore, the value of life goes down. People NEED to feel value in their life, so they start measuring themselves in terms of things they want but do not necessarily have or can control. This leads to a lot of negative emotions that, in the end, result in desperation and depression.

During wartime however, death being an on-going reality, the value of life goes up. A person is just happy to wake up another day, and that is what he looks forward to the night before. War minimizes our wants and expectations and makes it easier to be happier with our potions in life, and that makes depression less of a possibility, at the very least, because of trivial matters.

Furthermore, one of the depressing parts of life is suffering alone. Misery truly loves company if only to normalize one's own suffering. During peacetime, individuals suffer and that makes them feel lonely and unfortunate. During a war, when so many others are suffering as well, it becomes the norm to feel pain as well, making it more bearable.

All-in-all, war is a HUGE emotional distraction away from the less important matters in life. It also provides ongoing perspective about life that seems to dissipate during peacetimes. Into that void goes faulty values that can end up causing all kinds of unnecessary suffering that the mind treats as real. Not all brains, from which the emotions take their lead, are smart enough to know this on their own.

War has probably "cured" a lot of personal depressions in the past. The ongoing EMOTIONAL distraction eventually "rewires" the depressed person's brain until they get used to living without depression. War changes people, and often from people who CAN become depressed into those who can no longer become depressed.

Of course, few psychiatrists are going to prescribe war as means to end depression. Too dangerous. But the idea can certainly be applied: constant, major EMOTIONAL distraction over an extended period of time.

Whatever the activity is, it has to be CONSTANT, at least in the beginning. Otherwise, bad habits, which are hard to break, will push the person back into their negative frame of mind. Then they'll just experience ups-and-downs, as opposed to the extended period of up necessary to rewire the brain and build confidence in happiness.

It has to be a MAJOR emotional distraction, because it won't get a suffering person's attention otherwise. Suffering is a very strong emotional distraction, and it will take an even stronger one to snap a person out of it long enough to get their attention, or at least enough of it to pull them out of themselves.

The emotional distraction program also has to last for an EXTENDED PERIOD of time. Change does not come easy to people, unless it is shockingly dramatic, which can cause negative side effects, or over time. A person has to be away from their old self until it becomes only a memory which can fade over time, leaving room for a new self.

A wilderness program works this way. It takes a person out of their usual, more pampered environment, and throws them int a distant and rugged one. The person has to spend so much time dealing with the challenges of dealing with their most basic necessities that they lose all interest in trivial matters and pleasures.

And this is the way they live for a couple of weeks, perhaps even longer. It may be cheating a bit to know that survival is just one phone call away, but as long as they stay at it, it can be enough to full the brain and emotions to focus entirely on the here-and-now.

If they stick with the program long, they will be a different person at the end, stronger, healthier, more appreciative of the simple things in life and, therefore, less prone to psychological depression. If life throws one at them, they will look for ways to avoid, using the psychological survival skills they picked up while in the wilderness.

This is why it is no coincidence that some of the happiest people are social workers. Their work may be depressing, having to help others who cannot help themselves. But by constant comparison it is VERY difficult to not be appreciative of the simpler pleasures in life THEY have and those whom they help do not. Everyone else's suffering is a constant, major, and ongoing emotional distraction away from their own.

Is this the ULTIMATE way to deal with emotional distraction and wounded emotions? Of course not. These are just ways to teach us that we CAN deal with them, and learn to control them, as so many teach and as so many have done. These and similar means of emotional turnaround are purely for educational purposes only.

The ULTIMATE means of ruling over one's emotions to dictate approach to life? TRUTH. Mind over matter, right? Information, the theory goes, when known in detail and thoroughly, has the power to override ALL emotions, and courageously steer a person to emotional safety. If what you know isn't helping, then you don't know enough about it, or know it well enough.

For example, one person suffered from depression for some time and felt that he would NEVER get better. The fact that his family and friends all seemed happy and content only made him feel more hopeless...

In the course of looking for a way out, he eventually stumbled upon a book about personal tikun from a TORAH perspective. At first he began reading it only because it was interesting, but he kept reading it because it opened up his mind to an entirely different approach to life than he had learned growing up. And the more he read the more he realized that he was the one on the right track, not the society around him.

How did he know? Because the blissful lives they seemed to pursue and live did little to accomplish the tikun described by the book. People had grown materially, but very little spiritually, if at all. His suffering, he finally realized one day, made him spiritually-sensitive and open to growth. HE began to feel like the LUCKY one.

And that feeling on grew with time, especially as he learned to use life for spiritual growth. And then, all of sudden one day, he realized his depression had lifted. It no longer seemed relevant, seeming more like the faulty result of a mistaken perception about life. It took about a year and a half, but he had left depression and started feeling better about himself than he ever had.

It's a very important point. Perceptions are built upon assumptions, so if the assumptions are wrong then the perception will be wrong. We often meet people with completely different priorities than us, and wonder how such differences can exist. It takes but one discussion to find out that such differences exists because of a different set of assumptions about life.

The amazing thing is that, given how easy it is to make false assumptions about life, more people don't question theirs and check them against more reliable, time-tested assumptions. Instead people just assume that their perception of reality is the only that can exist, not really understanding how it is THEIR assumptions, which can easily be mistaken, that dictate their vision of reality.

A ba'al teshuvah is a good case in point. If he happens to be confronted by a religious person, he'll argue his anti-religion point with complete confidence. Until that is, he stops running out of answers for the questions, at which point he'll start to become flustered.

If he courageously sticks around long enough to hear the Torah's answer, and takes the time to come to terms with them, he will have an awakening. He might even be shocked about how he assumed certain things about life for the longest time without realizing in the slightest that they were erroneous.

If he pursues his new course of investigation even further, he will find his perceptions about reality, and his place in it, changing. As he one-by-one replaces a faulty assumption with a true one, his outlook will change quite naturally until, one day down the road, he finds himself accepting what had once been for him the contrary point of view.

Of course his friends and family who did not share his intellectual journey and remain in his old world, will not relate. How can they if they lack the knowledge to? Instead, they will assume that something bad happened to him, like losing his mind or something and, as a result, becoming religious and extreme.

Until that is, they start sharing his journey with him. Then he will find some who will crack early under pressure and avoid the discussion with him altogether, and some who will become fascinated and ask for more. Perhaps, they might even join him eventually on the "other side."

None of this will work, be it an emotionally-distracting activity, or an intellectual journey in search of higher truths, without WILL. You can trick a horse into ending up by the water, but it's a much taller order to get them to drink once it realize where it is. And USUALLY, unless a "horse" "drinks" of its own volition, nothing really changes AT ALL.

And it makes sense too. The world was not made for zombies. Though they exist in abundance, they are not the reason for Creation. They're just an unfortunate by-product of it. God made all of Creation, and it is WAY more vast than the physical one we talk about, for one reason and one reason only: FREE WILL.

And the amazing thing about free will is how just one free will decision at the right time and in the right way can change SO much. The ripple effect over time can be and often is dramatic, for good or for bad, of free will decisions. WHICH is determined by the moral basis of the decision that is being made.

If a person capitulates to the status quo, usually because it means not having to WILL to change it, then they can't expect better results. The only reason why we suffer is to "compel" us to USE our will. It's THE purpose of Creation.

It's like someone enrolling in a college course to become a professional, and ignoring the questions on the entrance exam because they just don't feel like doing them. "Studying is such bother," the person says, "and it is a lot easier to just daydream…"

"Then why did you sign up for the course?" we'd wonder to ourselves about this person. "You had to have known that they'd want you to study in advance and do well on the exam to get it! If you didn't, BOY were you misinformed!"

The same is true about life, except that we're not studying to get into college, but into the World-to-Come. Life is the entrance exam, which we have to study for so we can respond to its many challenges and difficulties with a good use of free will. Maybe we'll accomplish what we set out to do, maybe we won't. But we can NEVER fail as long as we employed our God-given attribute of will to the best of our ability. Do it enough times, and we get a LARGE portion in the World-to-Come.

The Talmud makes a curious statement:

Rebi Yehoshua ben Levi said: "Anyone who is joyful with their suffering brings salvation to the world, as it is said, 'through them, of old, we would be saved' (Yeshayahu 64:4)." (Ta'anis 8a)

It is one thing to accept one's suffering with joy, but save the world because of it?

How?

Why?

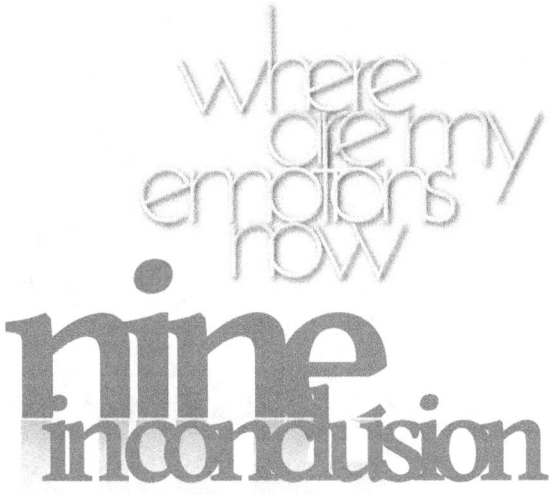

nine
in conclusion
where are my emotions now

WHERE ARE MY emotions now? I'd like to believe that they're here right now with me. But, it's two days until the Pesach Seder, and I am REALLY tired from the cleaning, OVERWHELMED (again) by the cost of making Pesach, and NERVOUS that I have missed something(s) from my list.

On quieter days, my writing is usually a good enough of an emotional distraction to draw my attention away from the outside world. I'm usually quite invested in my writing, intellectually AND emotionally. At this moment, not so much. It's hard to be focused when you're tried and emotionally scattered.

It's not comfortable. It's much nicer when I just sit down at the computer and the ideas flow through me and the keyboard to the screen. You feel one with everything, yourself, your work, with the world. What could be wrong with that?

Well, nothing per se. It's a gift. Any time you get something that you want but didn't earned, it's a gift. And the thing about gifts is:

> The one who hates gifts with live! (Mishlei 15:27)

which is too bad, because a LOT of people out there LOVE gifts.

In fact, more than life. For example, a group of young men was asked if they had a chance to EARN a billion dollars, or receive it for FREE, which would they choose. Just about everyone said, "Receive it for free!" even though they would end up with a billion dollars either way! The fact that they wouldn't have to work for it made it seem as if they were getting "more."

More of what?

Once while taking a bus from the Old City in Jerusalem, I got a free ride. I went to pay, but the machine to take my money and print me a ticket went on the blink. The driver tried to quick-fix it, but could not. So he told me, "You can sit down, and if you happen to remember on your next bus to pay, fine."

As I sat down, I felt slightly elated that I was getting a free ride. But I also realized that there was something wrong with the picture. I was enjoying a service that cost money, and I had enough to pay for it (about $1.50). Why should I feel good about not paying for something that didn't belong to me?

Especially since I am not a cheapskate. I don't like overpaying, but I don't mind paying what is fair. I also enjoy giving to others, and often more than I can afford? So what was with the buck-fifty that I was so happy to save on a bus that I really had to pay for?

The same thing that the guys thought they would get from a FREE billion dollars over one they could earn. There is something about getting things for FREE, as GIFTS, that makes life seem, well, so much RICHER, as if paying for things is a "rip off."

It seems that we have this sense of personal ENTITLEMENT. The world OWES us a living, and when it doesn't pay up, or worse, makes US pay instead, then we feel cheated. And how much more so does this seem like the case when so many others around seem to be receive a lot more than they give.

This is only true though if you think that this world is it, that there is nothing to follow. If you believe that this world is the "banquet hall," and not the "corridor" the rabbis speak about,[1] then why not have as much of it as you can? You live once, indulge.

Furthermore, if you think that man is just like the animals, just more sophisticated, then why struggle more than you have to? The motto is, "Minimize struggle, maximize gain," and have the best of both worlds.

As I rode my bus to the city, I realized that I seemed to have absorbed some of that philosophy into my worldview. Growing up in Western society had impacted my psyche, and I had come to love gifts just like the next person. It gave me such a chill.

It was a wake-up call for me. Good thing too, because as I evaluated how much that philosophy had entered my life, I also came to realize how much it had denied me some of it. How many times had I let need to struggle prevent me from going the extra mile, from giving me more TIKUN, and therefore, more LIFE.

Years later, I can't say that I have come to HATE gifts, freebies. Bad habits are hard to break,

---

[1] Pirkei Avos 4:16.

and upbringing is impossible consciously eradicate. But I can say that when comfort calls and the work at hand seems daunting, I have the capacity to WILL myself to confront it. I have come to better accept that it is MUCH better to have failed TRYING that it is to succeed without effort. The latter may give you the material success you FEEL like, but the former is what gives you the quality of life you really WANT.

And you save the world too. This is what the world was made for, for people who embrace the idea of tikun and commit themselves to it. Everyone else just flounders, making themselves historically unimportant. Even worse, they take the "course," but don't do the "work," and therefore, never really "graduate."

The Midrash says that the angels asked God, at Creation, "Why make man?"[2] After all, he was destined to sin and anger God so many times throughout history. It was a good question that God chose to wait a bit, thousands of years actually, before answering.

Fast forward to Shaul HaMelech. Two tragic miscalculations had cost him the kingship, which had been handed over to Dovid HaMelech. But he was still king, and he still had a battle to fight

---

2

against the Philistines who continued to hassle the Jewish nation.

Before going to battle however, Shaul contacted a dead Shmuel HaNavi to fight out his fate in battle.[3] The episode was questionable halachically, but it worked. Shmuel spoke to Shaul and told him the bad news: "Tomorrow you and your sons will join me."[4]

Some people, upon hearing such news, might have split the scene and hidden away. Others may have stayed to fight, but without the fight within them. Not Shaul HaMelech. He went to battle as the king of the Jewish people, courageous and as if he had never heard the news.

Shmuel's words of course came true: Shaul and all of his sons died in battle, Shaul himself by his own sword. But before he did, the Midrash says, God called together the Heavenly Hosts and told them, "You asked why I created man? Look down there! This man knows that he is destined to die in battle, AND with his sons as well, and yet he bravely fights on behalf of his nation with a complete heart! HE is the answer to your question!"

---

[3] 1 Shmuel 28.
[4] 1 Shmuel 28:19.

It is interesting how the man who made two major mistakes and got on God's bad side, so-to-speak, should be THE answer to the angels man-creation question. On the other hand, the Talmud says, when Dovid HaMelech wanted to praise God for his defeat of Shaul HaMelech, God told him to tone it down, telling him:

"Dovid, do you recite a song over the fall of Shaul? Had you been Shaul and he were Dovid, then I would have destroyed many Dovids before him. Although I decreed that Shaul's kingdom would not continue, as an individual he was far greater and more important!" (Moed Katan 16b)

Hmm. It's just one of those things in Judaism that seems to defy logic...until, that is, you look into the matter on a more Kabbalistic level. That's where the more incomprehensible aspects of Divine logic become less incomprehensible. Suffice it to say for now that Shaul, in spite of his errors, was a VERY great man, capable of being an example of what God values most in man.

The bottom line is we don't know the calculations of God. We only know what we know, and not always accurately either. We have desires and expectations, and we get impatient and jealous.

We get so wrapped up in this world that we forget there is another, more profound one coming. The yetzer hara keeps telling us, "Look here, look there...look everywhere except where it counts the most...at YOURSELF, at YOUR LIFE, past your body, THROUGH your eyes and at your SOUL." Talk about conspiracies!

But the main problem is not the yetzer hara. It was created to do what it does, and everyone one does it's much easier to excel at doing evil than it is to be righteous. That's the yetzer hara's home court advantage.

The main problem is that the one thing we were given to help us rout the yetzer hara, is left largely unused. Sure we use our brains for all those everyday mundane activities, and how to AVOID being good. But we don't use it enough to figure out how to be GREAT, how to take control of our will so that we can make the choices we WANT to make, not just the ones we FEEL like making.

No wonder our emotions are like wild stallions running loose over open terrain. Free will is the rope we need to lasso them in, so that we can saddle them and make them work for us, not the other way around. That's why I WILLED myself to continue writing and finish this chapter, the final one of this book.

And I am pleased to say that, after having done that, my emotions are currently on the same page as me, literally. And I can clearly say that what followed since I first began was the result of Heavenly help, as is everything in life. It's just that when your emotions are aligned with your will, you achieve a peace of mind that lets you SEE how God is involved in your life, making you succeed… even if you have yet to achieve lasting contentment.

But that's okay. Contrary to what it may look like out there in the world beyond your private one, this IS life.

Ups and downs.

Highs and lows.

Successes and failures.

Life and death.

Happiness and mourning.

And this is the way it is going to remain until the Messianic Era is in full swing, when free will is no more, and the chance to EARN more reward in the World-to-Come has ended, FOREVER. That's when we'll finally appreciate what we had and lost, and strangely, we may find ourselves yearning for "badder" times, and not better times, when free will made ALL the difference in the world to who we are and what we became.

So, tomorrow when you get out of bed in the morning, an act of will in itself, start your day by telling your emotions:

I have free will, and how I use it determines who I am, and how great I can be. Let it be that by the time I go to bed tonight, I will do so knowing that I used my will as many times as I could today, and in the most meaningful way possible. We'll have a MUCH greater day if we work in the same direction.

You don't feel like it? Good. It means you've got your emotions attention, and that is the FIRST step to knowing where they are.

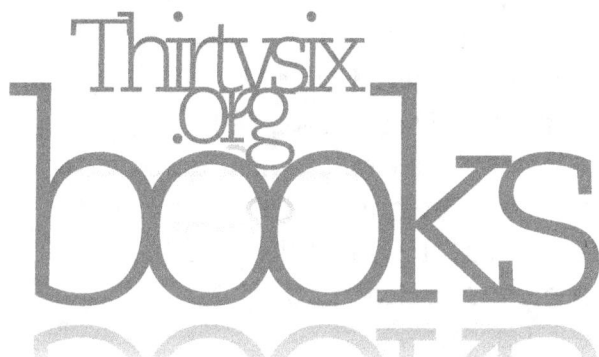

THE FOLLOWING TITLES are all the books written over the years. Some books may no longer be in print, but many are still available in either PDF or Kindle formats. Visit the Thirtysix.org OnLine Bookstore, or Amazon for more information, or to order online.

If you order using AmazonSmile, each purchase will generate a contribution for Thirtysix.org. You just have to designate "Thirtysix Org Inc." as your charitable organization of choice, and Amazon will take care of the rest.

The Unbroken Chain of Jewish Tradition, 1985
The Eternal Link, 1990
If Only I Were Wealthy, 1992
If Only I Understood Why, 1993
If Only I Could See the Forest, 1993
If Only I Could Stay, 1993

If Only Great Was Greater, 1993
The Y Factor, 1994
Life's A Thrill, 1994
No Atheists in a Foxhole, 1994
Changes that Last Forever, 1994
The Making of a Great Jewish Leader, 1994
Bereishis: A Beginning With No End, 1994
The Wonderful World of Thirtysix, 1995
Redemption to Redemption, 1997
The Big Picture, 1998
Perceptions, 1998
Not Just Another Scenario, 2001
At The Threshold, 2001
Anticipating Redemption, 2002
Sha'ar HaGilgulim, 2002
Hadran (Hebrew), 2004
Talking About The End of Days, 2005
Talking About Eretz Yisroel, 2005
The Physics of Kabbalah, 2006
Be Positive, 2007
Geulah b'Rachamim, 2007
God.calm, 2007
Just Passing Through, 2007
On The Same Page, 2007
The Equation of Life, 2007
No Such Victim, 2009
Survival in 10 Easy Steps, 2009
Not Just Another Scenario 2, 2011

All In Your Mind, 2011
The Light of Thirtysix, 2011
The Last Exile, 2011
Drowning in Pshat, 2012
Drown No More, 2012
Shas Man, 2013
The Mystery of Jewish History, 2013
Survival Guide For the End-of-Days, 2013
Deeper Perceptions, 2013
Chanukah Lite, 2015
The Hitchhiker's Guide to Armageddon, 2016
Purim Lite, 2016
Pesach Lite, 2016
The Torah Empowerment Seminar, 2016
Siman Tov (Hebrew), 2016
The Fabric of Reality, 2016
Addendum, 2016
Fundamentals of Reincarnation, 2017
Reincarnation Clarified, 2016
All About Energy, 2017
What Goes Around, 2017
The God Experience, 2017
What in Heaven, 2017
The God Experience, Part 2, 2017
The God Experience, Part 3, 2017
It's About Time, 2017
Need to Know, 2017
Perceptions, Volume 2, 2017

Once Revealed, Twice Concealed, 2017
The Art of Chayn, 2017
A Matter of Laugh or Death, 2018
Geulah b'Rachamim Program, V. 1, 2018
Geulah b'Rachamim Program, V. 2, 2018
Geulah b'Rachamim Program, V. 3, 2018
Point of Acceptance, 2018
See Ya, 2018
In Discussion: Bereishis, 2018
Reincarnation Again, 2018
A Separate Matter, 2018
In Discussion: Shemos, 2019
A Search for Self, 2019
A Search for Trust, 2019
In Discussion: Bamidbar, 2019
How It Might Play Out, 2019
In Discussion: Vayikra, 2019
Where Are My Emotions Now, 2019

For more information regarding any of these books or other projects, write to pinchasw@thirtysix.org, especially if you are interested in making a dedication in an upcoming publication.

essays, books, video, audio that which change the way you look at life—and history

www.ingramcontent.com/pod-product-compliance
Lightning Source LLC
Chambersburg PA
CBHW072147280526
45788CB00002B/794